Trains to the Lincolnshire Seaside

Volume Three

Cleethorpes

A. J. Lud

Published
Lincolnshire Wolds

GW00498785

Class B1 4-6-0 No 61316, carrying a 41A Sheffield Darnall shedplate on its smokebox door, leaves Cleethorpes with a returning excursion train in the late 1950s.

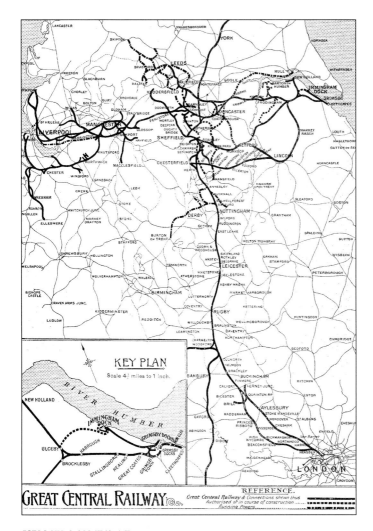

GREAT CENTRAL RAILWAY

REFERENCE.
Great Central Railway & Connections shewn thus
Authorised of in course of construction
Running Powers

KEY PLAN
Scale 4½ miles to 1 inch.

ISBN 978-0-9926762-4-7

The Lincolnshire Wolds Railway Society would like to thank Alf Ludlam and
Phil Eldridge for giving their time to compile this publication, to Dennis Lowe,
Graham Fenwick, Leyland Penn and Tony Jones for their contributions, and to
Allinson Print & Supplies for their support with the project.

Printed by Allinson Print & Supplies, Allinson House, Lincoln Way,
Fairfield Industrial Estate, Louth, Lincolnshire LN11 0LS

Issue 1. Autumn 2014.

CONTENTS

Introduction   1.

Arrival of the railway   3.

Holiday traffic   15.

Evening excursions and local traffic.   31.

The 1953 floods   39.

London excursions   41.

Present day   47.

The entrance to Cleethorpes station seen from the North Promenade on 5th May, 1953. The clock tower shows the time to be 7.15 am and the ornate refreshment room is seen in all its splendour. *Transport Treasury.*

THEATRE ROYAL

CLEETHORPES   Tel. No. 61223

The Premier Cinema and Variety Theatre in the District

SPECIAL HOLIDAY MATINEES
All the Best Stars and Latest Films are featured
See Weekly Advert for further details

VISIT THE ROYAL FOR PERFECT HOLIDAY ENTERTAINMENT

●

Also—DINE and DANCE at the

ROYAL CAFÉ

HIGH-CLASS CATERING   MODERATE CHARGES

ADJOINS STATION AND SEA

PARTIES ARE OUR SPECIALITY   *Accommodation for* 600

SERVICE   COMFORT   SATISFACTION

Write Resident Manageress for Tariff   Phone 61223

INTRODUCTION

The seaside resort of Cleethorpes is on the Lincolnshire coast where the Humber estuary meets the North Sea. The original parish of Clee included the inland present village of Clee and four separate hamlets, Weelsby, like Clee lay inland, but the others, Oole, Itterby and Thrunscoe were on the coast. The hamlets were known as the 'thorpes' of Clee. By the sixteenth century the name Cleethorpes was being used to describe Oole and Itterby, they were joined in the 19th century by Thrunscoe. Clee and a large part of Weelsby were absorbed into Grimsby.

In modern times as well as entertainment provided in the theatres, cinemas and dance halls, there were many entertainers who appeared in tented accommodation on the sands.

In 1935 Jimmy Slater, the country's leading female impersonator brought his "Super Follies" show to the sands, just opposite the station steps. In his beautifully dressed and presented little troupe was stage and TV "drunk", Freddie Frinton, who later made the TV series "Meet the Wife" with Thora Hird.

One of the highest paid entertainers pre-war was Madam Zillahl who was making £300 a week with her mind reading and future predictions act on the sands in 1939. The act would be introduced by her "barker", who sang "Oh Sweet Mystery of Life" in a Guiness-ravaged voice.

Jimmy Slater's "Super Follies" at Cleethorpes in the 1930s. Freddie Frinton is on the extreme left.

A 1910 postcard view of the Pier and Pavilion at Cleethorpes.

A postcard showing a pre-World War I view of Cleethorpes station from platform 1. The card was "Published by E.A. Schwerdtieger & Co. London E.C., printed at our works in Berlin".

ARRIVAL OF THE RAILWAY

The Great Grimsby & Sheffield Junction Railway (GG&SJR) was launched at a well-attended meeting at the Red Lion Hotel in Caistor on 28th October, 1844. It was resolved to construct a railway from Grimsby to Gainsborough. A further meeting in the Town Hall in Grimsby, on 6th November, considered three possible routes suggested by engineer John Fowler. The first alternative was via Caistor, the second via Brigg and the third via Market Rasen. The route via Brigg was approved with the resolution to build a branch from there to Market Rasen. Support was also expressed for the Sheffield & Lincolnshire Junction Railway, which would link the GG&SJR with the Sheffield, Ashton-under-Lyne & Manchester Railway, thus providing a continuous link between Grimsby and Manchester.

By the end of 1844 the GG&SJR had achieved an understanding with the Grimsby Haven company, which anticipated the formation of the Grimsby Docks Company (GDC). The GDC sought powers in the 1845 Session of Parliament to extend the docks at the same time as the GG&SJR secured its Act of Incorporation. By May 1845 estimates for the construction of the railway were:

Main line -	£389,929
Market Rasen branch -	£30,385
New Holland branch -	£27,730

G.N. 6698   5000   9 20   (18)
Great Northern Railway.
TO
Cleethorpes

The GG&SJR recieved Royal Assent on 30th June, 1845. The Grimsby to Gainsborough line was constructed by John Stephenson & Company and opened in three sections - Grimsby to Brocklesby on 1st March, Brocklesby to Brigg in November and Brigg to Gainsborough on 2nd April, 1849. Included in the first section was the New Holland line, which opened the same time as the East Lincolnshire line from Louth to Grimsby.

The companies which the Act of Incorporation of 27th July, 1846 brought together to form the Manchester, Sheffield & Lincolnshire Railway (MS&LR) were the Sheffield, Ashton-under-Lyne and Manchester Railway, the Great Grimsby & Sheffield Junction Railway, the Sheffield & Lincolnshire Junction Railway and the Grimsby Docks Company, the oldest progenitor and the company largely responsible for the early development of the commercial docks in the town. The latter company shared several directors with the GG&SJR - Lord Worsley, Richard Thorald, Michael Ellison, George Heneage and Richard Wall.

An Act of 26th June, 1846 authorised the GG&SJR to operate ferries across the River Humber from New Holland to Hull. Branch lines were also sanctioned between New Holland and Barton-on-Humber and from Grimsby to Cleethorpes, but the Cleethorpes proposals came to nothing.

The MS&LR were keen to extend their railway beyond Grimsby Docks to Cleethorpes, but it was not until 1855 that three route proposals were projected. All three were far from ideal and would have resulted in traffic chaos in Grimsby and Cleethorpes. They were all three wisely rejected.

The next proposal was in 1861, this projected line would run north from the East Marsh until it reached the coast and would then follow the shoreline to Cleethorpes station. The application to build the line was in the 1861 Session of Parliament. The single-track branch was opened on 6th April, 1863. Delay in the construction of the railway had been largely caused by difficulties with local landowners. It was one of the few MS&LR lines to be laid with creosoted sleepers, the company only used such sleepers on lines passing through sandy districts. The company's policy of using non-creosoted sleepers lasted until 1866 and the appearance of W. H. Stubbs as Company Engineer.

The original station at Cleethorpes had the main building on platform one, it still survives. After the doubling of the line, in 1874, plans were made to construct new buildings across the end of the platforms. The new station had six platforms and a turntable, installed near the signal box, its original diameter is unclear but its eventual size was 65 ft. The work was completed in 1880.

In the beginning the development of Cleethorpes was slow. The construction of the 1,200 ft long pier by the Cleethorpes Pier Company in 1873 had not intruded upon the rural feel of the place, with its cottages, shops and windmill. New Clee, the only intermediate station on the branch, was 1^1/$_2$ miles from Cleethorpes and was opened on 1st July, 1875. In the early 1900s a halt was built for dock workers at Fish Dock Road and was known as Riby Street Platform. It was used by dock workers who lived just outside Grimsby and travelled to work by train, there was no shelter on the platform.

L·N·E·R

EASONS

 ## HALF-DAY
Corridor Excursions

LONDON

(KING'S CROSS),
THURSDAY, April 19th,
(*Bookings from Skegness, Wainfleet and Firsby on April 19th only).

> LUNCHEON 3/- outward and SUPPER 2/6 on return will be
> provided on April 19th only, Dining Accommodation Limited.

SATURDAY, April 28th, 1928.
(†Bookings from Alford Town on April 28th only).

FROM			TIMES April 19th.	TIMES April 28th.	RETURN FARES, Third Class.	
			a m.	a.m.	s.	d.
CLEETHORPES	...	...	11 0	11 0		
GRIMSBY DOCKS	...	...	11 5	11 5	8	0
GRIMSBY TOWN	...	...	11 15	11 15		
LOUTH	...	...	11 35	11 35	7	6
†ALFORD TOWN	...	...	—	11 50	7	0†
*SKEGNESS	...	...	11 35	—	7	0*
*WAINFLEET	...	...	11 45	—	6	6*
*FIRSBY	...	...	12 0	—		
BOSTON	...	...	p.m. 12 25	p.m. 12 24	5	6
SPALDING	...	...	12 45	12 44	5	0
KING'S CROSS... arr.			2 40	2 40		

Passengers return from King's Cross on Saturday, April 28th at 11.50 p.m.
and on Thursday, April 19th, at 12·0 midnight.

EASONS ARRANGE DRIVES, MEALS, and supply THEATRE TICKETS Etc., in **LONDON** if desired·
☞ Intending Passengers are advised to BOOK IN ADVANCE.   MONEY instantly
REFUNDED on all TICKETS taken in advance and NOT USED.

Tickets can be obtained in advance at the Stations and at the Offices of the Organisers, and
Passengers requiring Meals should make EARLY application to—

EASONS, L·N·E·R AGENTS,
1, OLD MARKET PLACE, & 81, CLEETHORPE ROAD, GRIMSBY.

Passengers leave their train at Cleethorpes circa 1910. They are wearing their "Sunday best" clothes, which they will continue to wear, the men, their jacket, waistcoat and cap, even while sitting on the beach. This photo shows how close Cleethorpes station is to the North promenade.

The real development of Cleethorpes began in 1880 after the decision had been taken to enlarge the station. The Urban Sanitary Authority asked the MS&LR to preserve High Cliff for recreational purposes, the company agreed to apply to Parliament, "for powers to construct such works of protection as may preserve the cliff at Cleethorpes and may enable the land to be saved to be converted into a place of recreation with baths and waiting rooms". It was later agreed to extend the area of improvement to the lifeboat station at the east end of the town. On 18th July an Act granted the MS&LR the required powers. 17 acres of land, costing £1,670, were bought the following year, and, early in 1883, a start was made on the sea defences.

The railway company eventually took over the Pier Company by an Act of 4th July, 1884. The sum of £10,000 was spent on swimming baths, stalls for hire, refreshment rooms, a colonade, a restaurant and a photographic studio. The additional lighting for the promenade and gardens was in place for the public opening by Prince Albert Victor on 2nd July, 1885. Later improvements included a pavilion on the pier, more stalls, a grotto in the Cliff gardens and timber groynes. An extension to the sea wall was started in 1891. In May 1892 the MS&LR bought the 33 acres which made up the remaining stretch of the foreshore between Grimsby and Cleethorpes for £4,500.

By 1900 more than £100,000 had been spent on the development of Cleethorpes by the railway company. The resort was attracting up to 30,000 people a day by rail. Such was the importance of the resort as a money maker for the Company that during an outbreak of smallpox in Grimsby and New Clee in the spring of 1888 the MS&LR were forced to cancel excursions to both places. With the lucrative Whitsun holidays approaching the General Manager ordered that Cleethorpes would be served by its excursion trains but they would not stop at Grimsby and New Clee.

The Great Central railway (GCR) came into existence on 1st August, 1897, not by amalgamation but by merely a change of name. The GCR Official Album said of Cleethorpes, "Beyond Grimsby the line has been pushed to Cleethorpes, a village once inhabited by a few fishermen, but now changed by a unique effort of railway enterprise into the most crowded watering place in Lincolnshire.

"It is almost entirely the property of the GCR, who have built a massive sea wall, 65 ft wide, the inner side of which is a broad carriageway divided from the promenade by a low wall. A pier, switchback, public gardens and other places of entertainment have been built by the enterprise of the Company, and, in the summer, the town is thronged with excursionists from Yorkshire, Lancashire and the Midlands".

The ornate station clock tower, and the refreshment rooms to the right, help make up this wonderful early 1900s view of the promenade area at Cleethorpes.

This 1960s aerial view of Cleethorpes shows how close the station was to the foreshore. The six platforms can be seen just below the pier. The signalbox, demolished in 1985, and turntable stand opposite the gasholder with the water tower and Chapman's brick-pond in the foreground. The Big Dips, a big attraction at the end of the north promenade, is in the left foreground.

Ex-MS&LR 4-4-0 No 5684 prepares to depart Cleethorpes station with a local train bound for New Holland. LNER class D7 No 5684 was built in November 1891 and lasted until June 1939. *Lens of Sutton.*

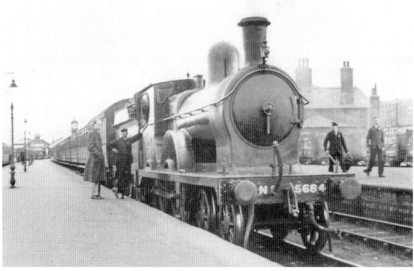

A friend of the photographer poses with the driver of class D7 4-4-0 No 5684 at platform 4 in the 1930s. The train was a local stopping service to New Holland. No 5684 was built in November, 1891 and was one of only two of the class remaining and allocated to New Holland, she was withdrawn in June 1939.

PIER PAVILION

FOR DANCING & MUSIC

◆

Don Twidale and his Band

DANCING DAILY

Afternoons, 3—5   -   Evenings, 7.30—11

Regular Special Late & Carnival Dances, Cabarets	Late Buses to all Parts on all occasions

CELEBRITY CONCERTS

EACH SUNDAY

with Britain's Premier Vocalists

See opposite page, weekly posters and programme for details

◆

PIER TOLL, 2d.

WEEKLY AND SEASONAL TICKETS ISSUED

Fishing from the Pier

COME TO THE PIER FOR HEALTH AND ENTERTAINMENT!

A very smart looking class K3 2-6-0 No 61897 passes beneath Fuller Street bridge and New Clee sidings with a returning excursion train in the late 1950s. Built for the LNER at Darlington in 1930 No 61897 was withdrawn from service in February 1962.

Lincoln-based D9 4-4-0 No 5113 is pictured on 26 May 1934 after running through Brocklesby station with the 3.10pm Cleethorpes to Penistone service. *T. E.. Rounthwaite.*

The view of a busy station seen from Cleethorpes signal box in the 1930s with class J2 0-6-0 No 3079 in platform 5; class J39 0-6-0 No 2700 in platform 4; J39 No 1269 in 3 and class B6 4-6-0 No 5416 in platform 2.

HOLIDAY TRAFFIC

There were three principal train flows into the resort which came together at Wrawby Junction, west of Barnetby. They came from, A. Sheffield via Doncaster and Scunthorpe, B. through Worksop and Retford via Gainsborough, and, C. through Lincoln via Market Rasen. The New Holland-Cleethorpes service, which joined the main line at Habrough, usually produced a couple of extras on peak Sundays, filled with day trippers from Hull via the Humber Ferry. A further possible route to Cleethorpes was over the East Lincolnshire line through Louth, but this was rarely used for day excursion traffic as it entailed a reversal at Grimsby Town, which was chaotic enough due to level crossings at both ends of the station.

The extensive New Clee sidings, alongside the main line, ran from Fuller Street to New Clee, covering most of the land between the railway and the bank of the Humber. They were built to handle coal traffic for the trawling fleet and fish trains as well as stabling for trip trains.

Fireman Dennis Lowe described working an August mid-week special from Chesterfield to Cleethorpes. Dennis and his driver, Arthur Liquerish, arrived at Colwick shed to begin their duties. "The notice board showed the loco for the day was No 61833, a class K3 2-6-0 "Jazzer". The engine was dirty and in poor condition, coal in the tender was just like dust. Not a good sign!

"We left the shed and ran light to Chesterfield to pick up ten bogies, around 310 tons. The route was new to both of us, so we were joined by a pilotman from Staveley GC depot for our trip to Cleethorpes.

"61833 did not steam well and the fire soon got very dirty. We made our way to the main line at Staveley Town station and on to Killamarsh Junction and Worksop, then over the GN main line at Retford to Gainsborough, where we stopped to take water and get up a full head of steam. On to Barnetby, Grimsby and Cleethorpes, where we arrived a little late, around mid-day.

"After pushing the stock back into the sidings the loco was uncoupled and turned, coaled (much better quality!), watered and the fire cleaned ready for the homeward journey. We later returned the coaches to the station ready for a 5.00 pm departure.

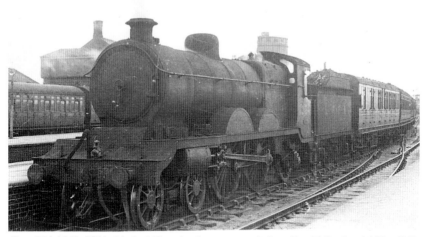

Class C4 4-4-2 No 5364 with the 6.10 pm local passenger train from New Holland on 9th May, 1946.
H. C. Casserley.

Harry Ellerby in the signal box at Cleethorpes.

"The run home was much better, the loco steaming well, and we arrived at Chesterfield to time. After dropping off the pilotman we put the bogies back in the sidings and ran light-engine up the bank to Heath Junction, joining the GC main line. We arrived back at Colwick some 12 hours after we left."

At Cleethorpes the signal box was north of the ends of the six platforms. Water columns were provided at platforms 1, 3 and 5. To the north of the box were six sidings that were used for excursion trains. The first train was moved into No 1 siding, next to the main line. Each siding held two trains, so the first train backed up to the top end of No 1 siding. The shunter hooked off the engine and came back with it behind the signal box. It was turned on the turntable and sent down siding No 6, which was kept clear for this purpose and sent down to Suggitts Lane signal box. This box had nothing to do with main line running and dealt only with the sidings between Cleethorpes and New Clee. The signal man at Suggitts Lane returned the engine to its train and moved it into New Clee Sidings, where it remained until time for its departure. Meanwhile specials continued to arrive. A second train would be backed into No 1 siding and a third to the top of No 2. Usually by the time No 3 siding was full and a train at the top end of No 4, No 1 siding would be empty. This procedure continued throughout the day. While this was happening ordinary trains would continue to arrive, usually at No 1 or 2 platforms in the summer. The engines were turned, put back on their trains, take water and be ready to leave. When the box was busy there could be as many as six trains moving at once.

Harry Ellerby worked at Cleethorpes as a signalman for 36 years until his retirement in 1960. "We had a different kind of problem during the winter fog. Sometimes it was so bad we couldn't see the station. If, for instance, I relieved my mate at six in the morning he would have to explain to me what the present situation was in the station. I would have to memorise the situation and act accordingly, with six platforms to contend with this could be quite complicated. The reason for this situation was because we had nothing in the box to indicate the state of things outside.

"There was an arrangement whereby if signalmen thought their box could justify a higher classification, and could prove it to the company, the box could be reclassified. This meant that a Class 3 box could be upgraded to a Class 2 and the signalmen could expect a wage increase of £10 a week. I had been at Cleethorpes about ten years when we decided to make an application to have the box made up to a Class 2. London agreed to send three inspectors to Cleethorpes, each of them allocated to a shift. Once the three shifts had been completed the inspectors returned to London. We had to wait a fortnight for the news that from 1934 Cleethorpes was a Class 2 box.

"Ten years later I persuaded my mates to have a go at getting the box made up to a Class 1. We informed London and were told the procedure would be the same as last time.

"About a week before the inspection I had a word with as many locomen as I could, most of them were from Immingham or Grimsby and we knew them well. The normal procedure was for them to come up the main line light engine and stop at the home signal from where they telephoned the box to tell us who they were, what train they had come to work and to ask what platform we wanted them in. We would then drop the engine onto its train and it was ready for departure. However, with the inspection in prospect I said to the locomen, "Don't think we've gone crackers, but when you come up light-engine you won't be put on your train straight away, we'll put you somewhere else first". This meant that the more we had to move them the more lever movements we made and the more marks we would be awarded.

"Our efforts were successful and the box made up to a Class 1. At the same time an electric diagram was installed above the levers in the box which showed us train movements and the situation in the station platforms.

"Five years before I retired Cleethorpes was made up to Special Class. We had become top class signal men and it was a marvellous way to end my railway career".

Graham Fenwick started his work as a signalman at Cleethorpes in the mid 1970s. "There were five platforms at the station that were all in use every day, six carriage sidings, a washing plant and fueling line, and a down siding which was known as the coal yard.

"There were four direct trains a day each way to Kings Cross, which were loco hauled, sometimes by Deltic class locomotives, which continued until the service was reduced to one train a day, worked by a HST set. The train was pushed by the loco from the platform to the carriage sidings so that the loco could run round the train for the return journey. When a Deltic was on the service the signal box would often shake when the driver opened up the throttle. On the night shift in those days eleven dmus were fueled, washed and serviced during the night."

Dick Dunnett was in charge of the Immingham men who acted as relief crews at Cleethorpes. "Behind the signal box was a building with a room used by the loco inspectors and twenty or so drivers and firemen. These men would meet the visiting specials and relieve the crews, who would do no more work until they took the train home in the evening. As soon as the train was empty and ready to back out of the station the relief men would notify the signal box via a telephone at the end of the platform and the disposal procedure would begin. They would water the engine, clean the fire and oil round before turning the engine on the turntable near the signal box. The engine and its coaches would be moved to New Clee Sidings until the time for its return journey. Each relief crew would deal with several engines during the course of their shift".

Cleethorpes signal box in the 1950s, the edge of the turntable is visible next to the signal.
F. A. Blencowe.

Oh we do like to be beside the seaside! A busy scene near "Wonderland" on the North Promenade.

The original Cleethorpes station buildings, the scene dominated by the huge water tank and its wooden cover. *R. K. Blencowe.*

Immingham-based class B1 4-6-0 No 61318 stands in platform 4 at Cleethorpes with the 6.35 pm to Manchester on 24th August, 1963. *R. E. Burdon.*

CLEETHORPES

A wooden Cleethorpes destination board. The reverse side reads "New Holland".

GCR "Large Director" Class D11/1 4-4-0 No 62660 "Butler Henderson" approaches Retford with a Cleethorpes-Manchester train on 19th July 1959. This engine is now restored to its original GCR livery as part of the National Collection.

GREAT CENTRAL RAILWAY

WHITSUNTIDE HOLIDAYS.
ONE TO EIGHT DAYS AT CLEETHORPES.

Commencing on Friday, May 17th, & Saturday, May 18th, and Every Day until Whit-Saturday, May 25th, 1907,

Dean & Dawson's Eight Day Return Tickets, First and Third Class, to

CLEETHORPES

Will be issued from the undermentioned Stations by all Trains at the following Fares, which will be available for return any day by any Train within Eight Days from the date of issue:—

STATIONS	Fares to CLEETHORPES and back within 8 days		STATIONS	Fares to CLEETHORPES and back within 8 days	
	1st s. d.	3rd s. d.		1st s. d.	3rd s. d.
Alexandra Park	16 0	8 0	Killamarsh	13 0	7 0
Altrincham and Bowdon	17 0	8 6	Kirkby and Pinxton	13 0	8 3
Ardwick	16 0	8 0	Lavenshulme	16 0	8 0
Ashbury's	16 0	8 0	Macclesfield (Central)	16 0	8 0
Ashton (P. P. or O. R.)	16 0	8 0	Manchester (London Bd. or Central)	16 0	8 0
Beighton	13 0	7 0	Marple	16 0	8 0
Belle Vue	16 0	8 0	Middlewood	16 0	8 0
Birch Vale	16 0	8 0	Mottram & Broadbottom	16 0	8 0
Bollington	16 0	8 0	Newpond	13 0	7 0
Bredbury	16 0	8 0	New Mills	16 0	8 0
Brooklands	17 0	8 6	Newton	16 0	8 0
Bulwell Common	13 0	8 3	Oldham (C. St. or G. Rd.)	16 0	8 0
Chesterfield	13 0	8 3	Old Trafford	16 6	8 3
Chorlton-cum-Hardy	16 0	8 0	Oughty Bridge	14 0	7 0
Crowden	16 0	8 0	Park Bridge	16 0	8 0
Darnall (for Handsworth)	13 0	7 0	Penistone	14 0	7 0
Deepcar	14 0	7 0	Pilsley	13 0	8 3
Dinting	16 0	8 0	Poynton	16 0	8 0
Dukinfield	16 0	8 0	Reddish	16 0	8 0
Dunford Bridge	16 0	8 0	Romiley	16 0	8 0
Eckington and Renishaw	13 0	7 6	Rose Hill	16 0	8 0
Fairfield (for Droylsden)	16 0	8 0	Sale & Ashton-on-Mersey	17 0	8 0
Fallowfield	16 0	8 0	Sheepbridge and Brimington	13 0	8 0
Glossop	16 0	8 0	Sheffield (Victoria)	13 0	7 0
Godley	16 0	8 0	Stalybridge	16 0	8 0
Gorton	16 0	8 0	Staveley Town	13 0	7 6
Grassmoor	13 0	8 3	Staveley Works	13 0	7 6
Guide Bridge	16 0	8 0	Stretford	16 6	8 3
Hadfield	16 0	8 0	Strines	16 0	8 0
Hayfield	16 0	8 0	Tibshelf	13 0	8 3
Haslehead	16 0	8 0	Timperley	17 0	8 6
High Lane	16 0	8 0	Wadsley Bridge	14 0	7 0
Huddersfield	16 0	8 0	Woodhead	16 0	8 0
Hucknall Town	13 0	8 3	Woodhouse	13 0	7 0
Hyde	16 0	8 0	Woodley	16 0	8 0
Hyde Junction	16 0	8 0	Wortley	14 0	7 0
Hyde Road	16 0	8 0			

ROUTES BY WHICH PASSENGERS CAN TRAVEL. { 1. Via Retford and Brigg; { 2. „ Penistone, Doncaster and Elsham;

Passengers must satisfy themselves before starting that they can complete their journey according to the route of the Ticket the same day, and the Company will not be accountable for any loss or inconvenience which may arise from delays or detentions.

FOR CONDITIONS UPON WHICH EXCURSION TICKETS ARE ISSUED, SEE NOTICES EXHIBITED AT THE STATIONS, AND THE COMPANY'S AGENCIES.

Tickets and Bills of the above, and general information respecting all Great Central Excursions, can be obtained any time in advance at any of the Company's Booking Offices and Stations; DEAN & DAWSON'S EXCURSION OFFICES, 49, Piccadilly, Manchester; 2, Mumps, Oldham; 7, Haymarket, Sheffield; 49, New Street, Huddersfield; and the Usual Agents.

All information as to Excursion Trains can be had on application to Mr. GEO. J. GIBSON, District Superintendent, Great Central Railway, London Road Station, Manchester, or from any of Messrs. Dean & Dawson's Excursion Offices.

Marylebone Station
London, N.W., April, 1907.

SAM FAY, General Manager.

M.D. 239   "GLOBE" Printing and Bookbinding Co., Stockport.   -/14,800

A Dean & Dawson's handbill advertising holiday excursions to Cleethorpes in the early years of the Great Central Railway.

BRITISH EMPIRE
AUTUMN
EXCURSIO
WILL
LOND

On Mondays, 21st Sep
for 6, 8,

Available for return on Saturday followi
Monda

On Saturdays, 26th Se
for 4, 8

Available for return on Tuesday followi
Satur

FROM

CLEETHORPES ....
GRIMSBY (Docks) ....
GRIMSBY (Town) ....
WALTHAM ....
NORTH THORESBY ....
MABLETHORPE ....
SUTTON-ON-SEA ....
LOUTH ....
ALFORD TOWN ....
BURGH-LE-MARSH ....
SKEGNESS ....
WAINFLEET ....
SPILSBY ....
FIRSBY ....
HORNCASTLE ....
WOODHALL SPA ....
WOODHALL JCN. ....
BOSTON ....
GAINSBORO' (Lea Road) ...
LINCOLN ....
SLEAFORD ....
arr. KING'S CROSS ....

A.—Due King's Cross, 1.35 p.m
King's Cross 5.10 p.m.

* On Saturday, 26th September
King's Cross 8.10 p.m.

For Return Arrangements

London, August, 1925.
6,000. 10/9/25.

**Many excursions also
as this 1925 LNER har**

**A selection of local
Edmondson railway tickets
from the LNER era.**

BITION—Wembley

URSIONS

TICKETS
TO
N (KING'S CROSS)

to 26th October incl.
DAYS
lowing, Saturday week following and
.

to 31st October incl.
DAYS
lowing, Monday week following and
ng.

re Times.	Return Fares. Third Class.	
p.m.	s.	d.
2 30	26	3
2 40	26	0
3 0	26	0
2 36	25	3
2 46	24	9
3 31	23	0
3 38	22	6
3 24	23	6
3 49	21	9
4 3	22	0
3 20	22	0
3 34	21	0
3 30	21	0
4 11	20	6
3 45	21	9
3 55	20	9
4 31	20	0
5 12	18	0
	24	0
3B 20	21	9
1D 48	18	9
8* 50		

ng's Cross 6.15 p.m. D.—Due

rboro' (Nth.) 6.37 p.m. due

Issue, etc., see back.

R.4699/B.

from Cleethorpes
s.

PLEASE RETAIN THIS BILL FOR REFERENCE   L210/A

RAIL & ROAD

BRITISH RAILWAYS (L.M. REGION)

AND

MIDLAND "RED"

SEASIDE EXCURSIONS

FROM

ELLISTOWN, BURBAGE, WHETSTONE FLECKNEY, KIRBY MUXLOE STONEY STANTON and
BARROW-ON-SOAR DISTRICTS

TO

CLEETHORPES

ON

MONDAY, AUGUST 7th & THURSDAY, AUGUST 10th
1950

THE 'BUSES WILL BE SPECIALLY LABELLED "ROAD-RAIL EXCURSION" AND PASSENGERS MAY JOIN AT THE USUAL STOPPING PLACES.

RETURN ARRANGEMENTS
PASSENGERS RETURN SAME DAY BY THE TRAINS SPECIFIED. MIDLAND "RED" OMNIBUSES WILL AWAIT THE ARRIVAL OF THE EXCURSIONS AT LEICESTER (CENTRAL) AND CONVEY THE PASSENGERS HOME.

THROUGHOUT ROAD and RAIL

RETURN 14/- FARE

CHILDREN under three years of age, free ; three years and under fourteen, half-fares.

CONDITIONS OF ISSUE
Day, Half-day and Evening tickets are issued subject to the conditions applicable to tickets of these descriptions as shown in the Bye-Laws and Regulations, General Notices, Regulations and Conditions exhibited at stations, or where not so exhibited, copies can be obtained free of charge at the station booking office.
For LUGGAGE ALLOWANCES also see these Regulations and Conditions.

TICKETS MAY BE OBTAINED IN ADVANCE from the Agents named on the other side and at adjacent stations ; and in order to facilitate arrangements and avoid disappointment ADVANCE BOOKING IS DESIRABLE.

TICKETS MAY ALSO BE OBTAINED ON THE SPECIAL 'BUSES

Further information will be supplied on application to Stations, Agencies, or to Mr. H. TANDY, District Commercial Superintendent, Leicester. Telephone 5542, Extn. 40

August, 1950
E.R.O. 53301

BRITISH RAILWAYS

(PRT/568)

London Midland Region

(SEE OVER)

10,500 H.   Staffords. Netherfield.

Midland Red road-rail seaside excursions were popular well into the British Railways era.

Britannia 70013 "Oliver Cromwell" at Cleethorpes on Saturday 3rd March, 2012 with a "Lincolnshire Poacher" railtour. The "Brit" had an extended stay in the resort after suffering a broken piston ring. *L. Penn*

Class 47 No 47786 arrives at Platform 3 with the coaching stock for a West Coast Trains day trip from Cleethorpes to Edinburgh on Saturday 22 September, 2012.

An elegant ex-MS&LR class D7 4-4-0 No 5687, in immaculate condition, passes Littlefield Lane after leaving Grimsby Town station with a Cleethorpes-New Holland train in 1930. In 1921 ten members of the class were at Immingham and were used to work services between Cleethorpes, Grimsby, Immingham Dock, New Holland and Barton-on-Humber. They were used extensively on stopping services in Lincolnshire, which involved much tender first working. The footplate crews complained of the lack of protection from the elements and the majority of the class were fitted with weather boards on the tenders as witnessed here. *F. R. Hebron.*

<LNER> **CLEETHORPES** <LNER>
IT'S QUICKER BY RAIL
FREE HOLIDAY ANNUAL FROM ANY LNER OFFICE OR AGENCY OR FROM PUBLICITY MANAGER, R.P. TOWN HALL, CLEETHORPES

On 2nd October, 1965 class 7P Britannia 4-6-2 No 70012 "John of Gaunt" being turned on the turntable at Cleethorpes, prior to taking a RCTS railtour to New Holland and Barton-on-Humber. C. J. Paine.

Class B1 4-6-0 No 61204 stands in platform 5 at Cleethorpes at 9.35 am with a summer excursion in the late 1950s. Built by the North British Locomotive Company in June 1947, No 61204 was withdrawn in November 1965.

Holiday Railway Facilities

TO CLEETHORPES

MONTHLY RETURN TICKETS at about a penny a mile third class, minimum fare 2/6 (1st class approximately 50 per cent. higher than 3rd class, minimum fare 3/9), are issued from everywhere to Cleethorpes by any train any day. The tickets are available outward or return on any day within a calendar MONTH from day of issue, break of journey being allowed in each direction at any intermediate station. CHILDREN under 14 years HALF-FARES. Luggage will be conveyed free up to 150 lbs. for each first class and 100 lbs. for each third class ticket, or it may be sent in advance for 2/- per package, including collection, conveyance and delivery.

SPECIMEN MONTHLY RETURN TICKET FARES TO CLEETHORPES

From	1st Class	3rd Class	From	1st Class	3rd Class
BOLTON ...	29/11	19/11	MIDDLESBROUGH ...	33/2	22/1
BIRMINGHAM	35/6	23/8	NEWCASTLE ...	42/6	28/4
CHESTER ...	36/3	24/2	NORTHAMPTON ...	33/2	22/1
DERBY ...	25/3	16/10	NORWICH	35/11	23/11
HALIFAX ...	20/2	13/5	NOTTINGHAM ...	21/8	14/5
HUDDERSFIELD	21/8	14/5	OLDHAM ...	24/6	16/3
LEEDS	15/9	10/6	OXFORD	44/11	29/11
LEICESTER ...	28/0	18/8	RUGBY	34/8	23/1
LONDON ...	41/9	27/10	SHEFFIELD	19/3	12/10
MANCHESTER	26/9	17/10	WOLVERHAMPTON	35/11	23/11

During the season April—October, Weekly Holiday Season Tickets will be issued on demand from Cleethorpes, covering the following areas :—

1. Cleethorpes and Grimsby, Gainsboro', Lincoln, Boston, Skegness and Louth.

2. Cleethorpes and Grimsby, Doncaster, Bridlington, Hull, Hornsea and Withernsea.

These Season Tickets will be available for an unlimited number of journeys by any train, and the charge for each separate area will be 15/9 first class, and 10/6 third class, children under fourteen years of age, half-price.

Tickets will also be issued for Dogs and Bicycles accompanying holders of Weekly Holiday Season Tickets, at owner's risk, at a charge of 2/8 each for Dogs, and 5/3 each for Bicycle, per week.

Numerous day and half-day excursion trains are run to Cleethorpes throughout the season, and these trips afford a very cheap means of travel for the purpose of booking up the holiday accommodation. Further details can be obtained at any L.N.E.R. Station, Office, or Agency, or from the Passenger Manager, Liverpool Street Station, E.C.1.

Boston-based class K2 2-6-0 No 61728 backs its train towards Cleethorpes station from New Clee Sidings, ready for its return journey, passing under Fuller Street bridge, whilst class B1 4-6-0 No 61126 begins its homeward trip in the 1950s. The K2 was built at Doncaster in April 1913, one of the original batch of ten class K1 engines designed by Nigel Gresley. Later converted to class K2 by the LNER and withdrawn in December 1960. The B1 was built by the North British Locomotive Company in February 1947 and withdrawn in September 1963.

A young admirer stands alongside Immingham-based Britannia class 4-6-2 No 70036 "Boadicea" waiting departure from Platform 3 at Cleethorpes with a London bound excursion.

Cleethorpes station circulating area, booking office and ticket windows. The date on the back of this Civil Engineers Office, British Railways, Eastern Region photo gives the date as 8th August, 1951, although the posters on the wall near the ticket window are headed "London and North Eastern Railway".

EVENING EXCURSIONS & LOCAL TRAFFIC

The LNER ran evening excursions from places like Lincoln, Retford and Doncaster which allowed people to spend a few hours at the seaside. The fares were cheap and the trips were well patronised. There were, at times, as many as twelve evening excursions; the trains arriving as the daytime specials were leaving on their homeward journeys. The following list of evening departures from Cleethorpes on Sunday 13th June, 1958 gives an idea of the amount of traffic being dealt with.

Time	Platform	Stations
5.10	6	Mansfield, Sutton-in-Ashfield, Hucknall.
5.20	5	Worksop, Whitwell.
5.30	4	Scunthorpe, Althorpe, Crowle, Medge Hall, Thorne, Stainforth, Barnby Dun, Doncaster.
5.36	3	Howsham, North Kelsey, Moortown, Market Rasen, Wickenby, Snellend, Langworth, Reepham, Lincoln.
5.43	2	Grimsby Docks, Scunthorpe, Althorpe, Crowle, Medge Hall, Thorne, Stainforth, Barnby Dun, Doncaster, Conisborough, Mexborough, Kilnhurst, Rotherham, Sheffield.
5.50	5	Worksop, Whitwell, Elmton & Creswell.
5.55	4	Ordinary train to Doncaster.
6.00	3	South Elmsall.
6.13	2	South Elmsall.
6.20	-	Kiverton Bridge, Woodhouse.
6.25	1	Ordinary train to Manchester (London Road).
6.32	6	Ordinary train to New Holland and Hull Corporation Pier.
6.39	4	New Holland and Hull Corporation Pier.
6.54	3	Bradford.
7.00	2	Castleford.
7.07	5	Wombwell.
7.14	4	Fitzwilliam Hare Park.
7.21	1	Sheffield only.
7.28	6	Wombwell.

Time	Platform	Stations
7.35	3	Sheffield, Wadsley Bridge.
7.50	2	Nottingham, Beeston, Long Eaton, Stapleford, Trowell, Ilkeston, Langley Mill, Pye Bridge, Alfreton, Westhouses, Clay Cross.
7.57	5	Thorne, Stainforth, Barnby Dun, Doncaster, Rossington, Bawtry.
8.04	1	Chesterfield.
8.11	4	Fitzwilliam Hare Park.
8.18	3	Fledborough, Tuxford, Ollerton, Edwinstowe, Warsop, Shirebrook, Langwith, Elmton & Creswell, Clowne, Chesterfield.
8.25	2	Conisborough, Mexborough, Swinton, Kilnhurst, Rotherham.
8.32	5	Retford, Worksop, Shireoaks, Kiverton Park, Kiverton Bridge, Woodhouse, Darnall.
8.39	1	Conisborough, Mexborough, Swinton, Kilnhurst, Rotherham.
8.46	4	Barnetby, Elsham, Appleby, Scunthorpe.
9.18	3	Wath, Wombwell, Dovecliffe, Birdwell, Chapeltown, Grange Lane, Meadow Hall.
9.30	2	Hucknall, Bulwell, Radford, Nottingham.
9.40	4	Ordinary train to New Holland, no boat connection.

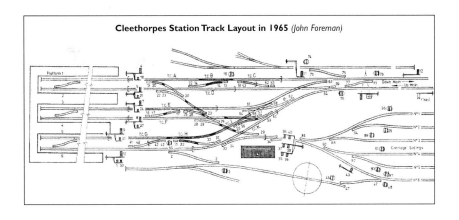

Cleethorpes Station Track Layout in 1965 (John Foreman)

In the early evening of 28th June, 1959 ex-GCR "Director" 4-4-0 No 62668 "Jutland" backs its empty stock into Cleethorpes station, over Suggitts Lane crossing. Other footplate crews are walking to New Clee sidings to collect their engines for the homeward journey.

Class D11 4-4-0 No 62666 "Zeebrugge" approaches Great Coates station with a Cleethorpes bound excursion during the late 1950s. At least five train spotters are in evidence. Great Coates signal box was built in 1884 and had a 39 lever frame. It remained in use until October 1987. No 62666 was a GCR Large Director built in October 1922 and finally withdrawn in December 1960. *R. B. Parr.*

Sheffield Darnall based class D11 4-4-0 No 62670 "Marne" works an excursion train through Brocklesby bound for Cleethorpes. "Marne" was the last engine built for the GCR, entering service a few days before the 1923 grouping. *N. E. Stead.*

A work-stained class B1 4-6-0 No 61212 stands in platform 6 at Cleethorpes with a passenger train in February 1956. Built by the North British Locomotive Company in July 1947 and withdrawn in November 1964. *R. K. Blencowe.*

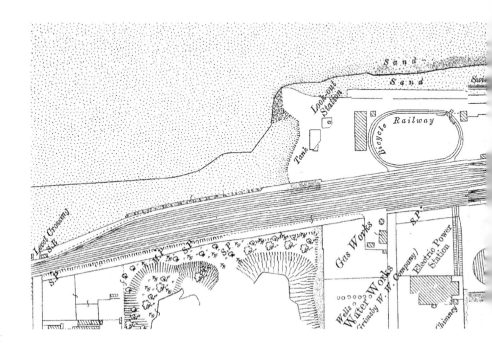

A relief crew fireman moves coal forward in the tender of visiting ex-LMS "Black Five" 4-6-0 No 44690.

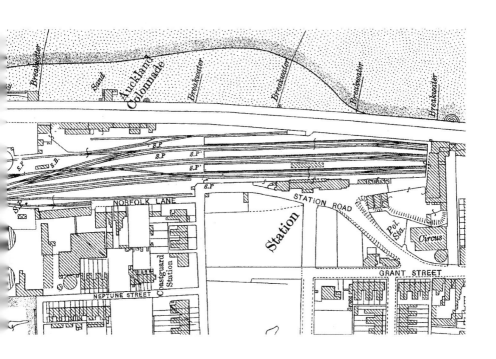

The aftermath of the 1953 floods on the section of track between Cleethorpes station and Suggitts Lane crossing. The sea crossed the line and engulfed the streets alongside the railway. *E. Fearnley.*

A smart-looking Immingham based class B1 4-6-0 No 61142 works a Cleethorpes-Kings Cross passenger train through Hitchin in 1958. No 61142 was at Immingham for over ten years and was built by Vulcan Foundry in April 1947 and withdrawn in September 1963.

1953 FLOODS

1953 was a year of mixed fortunes, Mount Everest was conquered by Edmund Hilary and Sherpa Tensing, Stanley Matthews finally won an FA Cup winners medal and the Coronation of Queen Elizabeth II all followed a disastrous start to the year. On the evening of 31st January a storm surge in the North Sea caused flooding and destruction along the east coast of England, from the Humber to the Straits of Dover, with the loss of 700 lives. Compared to Mablethorpe, Sutton-on-Sea and Ingoldmells, Cleethorpes escaped relatively lightly.

The sea broke the sea wall between Fuller Street and Suggitts Lane, damaging houses in the Fuller Street, Manchester Street and Oliver Street areas. I can remember watching the sea working its way down Fuller Street, crossing Grimsby Road and progressing down Elliston Street where it stopped, about 20 yards short of my house. The north promenade sea wall was breached in several places and damage caused to Wonderland, amusement arcades and shops and cafes.

The cost of the damage in Cleethorpes was estimated at £100,000. Work on repairing the damage and preparing the town for the new holiday season was the number one priority. Further damage was caused to the railway and embankment, around Suggitts Lane, the following March. However, by 1955 things had returned to normal and the resort enjoyed a very successful year. Nineteen trip trains arrived on Easter Monday, twenty specials arrived on the August Bank Holiday and the Bathing Pool admitted over 7,000 people in a single day.

HANCOCK'S
FAMOUS
BEACH AMUSEMENTS
NORTH PROMENADE

The "Palace of Pleasure"
is situate on the Sands nearly opposite the Station

Extensive COVERED-IN AREA provides an ideal
Playground for the Children in inclement weather

●

CAFÉ OVERLOOKING SEA   SPECIAL 1/- FISH TEAS

PARTIES CATERED FOR

CLEANLINESS, CIVILITY, SERVICE—**OUR MOTTO**

●

Proprietors - - **J. R. HANCOCK & SON, LTD.**

Regd. Office : " Kandylea," Elm Road, Cleethorpes

40

LONDON EXCURSIONS

As well as excursions working into Cleethorpes, special excursions, working initially from Grimsby, but after 1924, from Cleethorpes, were an important feature during the LNER period. They were usually run on Thursdays, which was half-day closing in Grimsby and Cleethorpes, and Saturdays. The excursions offered a morning, afternoon and evening in London. They left Cleethorpes at 7.00 am and arrived at Kings Cross at 10.30 am. The return trip left Kings Cross at Midnight. The excursions were run by the LNER and the Grimsby travel agency Easons and began in 1908.

Easons Travel Agency was founded by James Eason in 1901. At the end of World War 1 it was appointed the agency for the Canadian Government's immigration scheme and handled the transport arrangements for those who decided to emigrate to Canada. James Eason died in 1923 but his company continued in business until after World War 2.

The GNR sent an engine from Peterborough to work the specials, the LNER decided this was not a very efficient practice and decided to use Immingham based engines instead. This was an interesting decision in that it meant that former GCR engines would be working over the old GNR system into Kings Cross.

The trains were always popular. Eason's excursions differed from the usual excursions offered by railway companies, which usually used available stock, often lacking toilet facilities. Easons provided comfortable coaching stock, guaranteed seats and meals were served in both directions. The prices were reasonable and within the reach of ordinary families.

One of the biggest undertakings dealt with by Easons was the organising of 15 special trains to take Grimsby Town Football Club supporters to Huddersfield, to watch town play Arsenal in the 1936 FA Cup semi-final.

Two Immingham drivers, Sid Cleaver and Bill Croft had the road knowledge to work the specials, the idea was that they would work alternate shifts. They were joined in 1930 by drivers Paul Leake and Fred East, partly due to the popularity of the trips and partly in anticipation of the impending retirement of Messrs Cleaver and Croft.

The first appearance of an Immingham GCR engine at Kings Cross was on Saturday 29th September, 1923. The engine was a class B3 4-6-0 No 6169 "Lord Faringdon", in immaculate condition. GCR engines continued to work the excursions until 1939. The B3s were the first choice of engines for the trips. In 1924 class B7s Nos 5469, 5482 and 5484 arrived at Immingham and were ideal engines for the London excursions. When No 5482 worked into Kings Cross on Saturday 24th May, 1924, it was the first time a B7 had been seen there.

In 1933 class B2s appeared in the form of No 5426 "City of Chester", 5422 "City of Manchester", 5423 "Sir Sam Fay" and later 5428 "City of Liverpool", they had no problem working the eleven coaches of the London Specials.

Traffic working to and from Cleethorpes from the west was affected by problems at Grimsby Town station, which was restricted by the presence of level crossings at each end of the station. Working from Cleethorpes the line crossed Garden Street crossing, at the other end of the station was Wellowgate crossing. Space was so limited betwen the two crossings that the accommodation of any train of more than seven coaches in any platform interfered with connections to one or more of the adjacent roads.

Congestion problems at Town station with the flow of traffic from Doncaster, Sheffield, New Holland, Lincoln, Boston, Peterborough and elsewhere, was further complicated in the summer months by the passage of heavy day excursions bound for Cleethorpes.

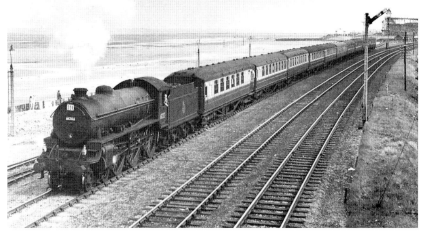

A class B1 4-6-0, No 61388 moves out of Cleethorpes with a return excursion train on 4th September, 1955.

Class BI 4-6-0 No 61151 awaits departure with the 3.59 pm passenger train to Sheffield on 30th August, 1956. Built at Vulcan Foundry in April 1947 No 61151 survived until September 1962. *R. M. Casserley.*

Healing station, between Habrough and Grimsby, witnessed what would have been a rare entry into the local spotters notebooks on 18th June, 1961, namely the passage of a Castleford-Cleethorpes excursion hauled by an ex-LMS 2-6-0 No 42963. *J. Willerton.*

Excursion trains and engines stabled in New Clee Sidings in the 1950s. Left to right, three class B1 4-6-0s No 61165, 61377 and 61230; class D11 4-4-0 No 62668 "Jutland"; class K3 2-6-0 No 61824; class B1s No 61208 and 61231; class K3 No 61803 and class D11 No 62660 "Butler Henderson".

Ex-LMS "Black Five" class 4-6-0 No 44792 passes New Clee Sidings on 16th August, 1959 with an excursion train for Cleethorpes. *J. Willerton.*

Nearing the end of steam traction at Cleethorpes, two English Electric Type 3s and a Derby Sulzer Type 2 wait at the head of excursion trains near Suggits Lane on 27th July, 1965. Two grimy class B1 4-6-0s can be seen near the Big Dips. *R. Hockney.*

PRESENT DAY

After World War 2 the LNER new Works Programme included £500,000 for improvements at Cleethorpes station. The buildings there were extensively modernised in 1965. The track layout was remodeled in 1985 and the number of available platforms reduced from six to five.

The massive reduction in the number of fish trains using the east side of Grimsby's Royal Dock and of excursions to Cleethorpes during the 1960s saw the end of New Clee Sidings; today nothing remains of them.

British Rail looked closely at its options, one of which was closure of the Cleethorpes branch. However the line remains open, with a cross country link to Manchester Airport. It was singled in 1985 at a cost of £1.2 million.

The branch continues to make its own history. The original station and its successor survive, as reminders of summer weekends when one could witness a terminus station working at its best, and watch the arrival of LNER "B1" 4-6-0s, "K2" and "K3" 2-6-0s, "D11" 4-4-0s, "J11" and "J39" 0-6-0s, the occasional "V2" 2-6-2 and "B12" and "B17" 4-6-0s. From the LMS came "5MT" 4-6-0s, Hughes Fowler 2-6-0 "Crabs", "Jubilee" 4-6-0s and a couple of rarities in the form of Stanier "5MT" 2-6-0 and "4P Compound". BR Standard types were regular vistors, particularly the "5MT" 4-6-0s and the occasional "Britannia" Pacific in the early 1960s.

THE CLEETHORPES COAST LIGHT RAILWAY

The Cleethorpes Miniature railway was laid at $10^1/_4$" gauge in 1948 and was converted to $14^1/_2$" in 1972. The present day 15" gauge was introduced in 1994. For many years it was owned by the local authority but by 1990 it was quite rundown. The lease was taken over by Chris Shaw and the name changed to the Cleethorpes Coast Light Railway. Under his direction and supported by volunteers the railway was revitalized. Extensions in 2000 and 2007 more than doubled its length to two miles. A lottery grant in 2002 secured the Sutton Miniature Railway collection of locomotives and rolling stock, which had been in store since 1962.

The sale of the Cleethorpes Coast Light railway was, announced on 27th May, 2014, the new owners are John Kerr and Peter Bryant.

Severn-Lamb "Rio Grande" 2-8-0 stands at the original Kingsway Station on the Cleethorpes Coast Light Railway.

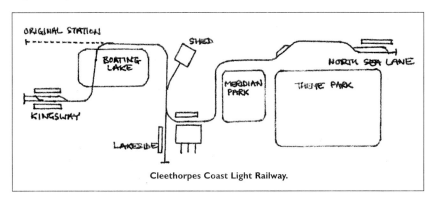

Cleethorpes Coast Light Railway.

Two more publications in the "Trains to the Lincolnshire Seaside" series...

Volume One:
Mablethorpe &
Sutton-on-Sea
Price £6.95

Volume Two:
Skegness
Price £6.95